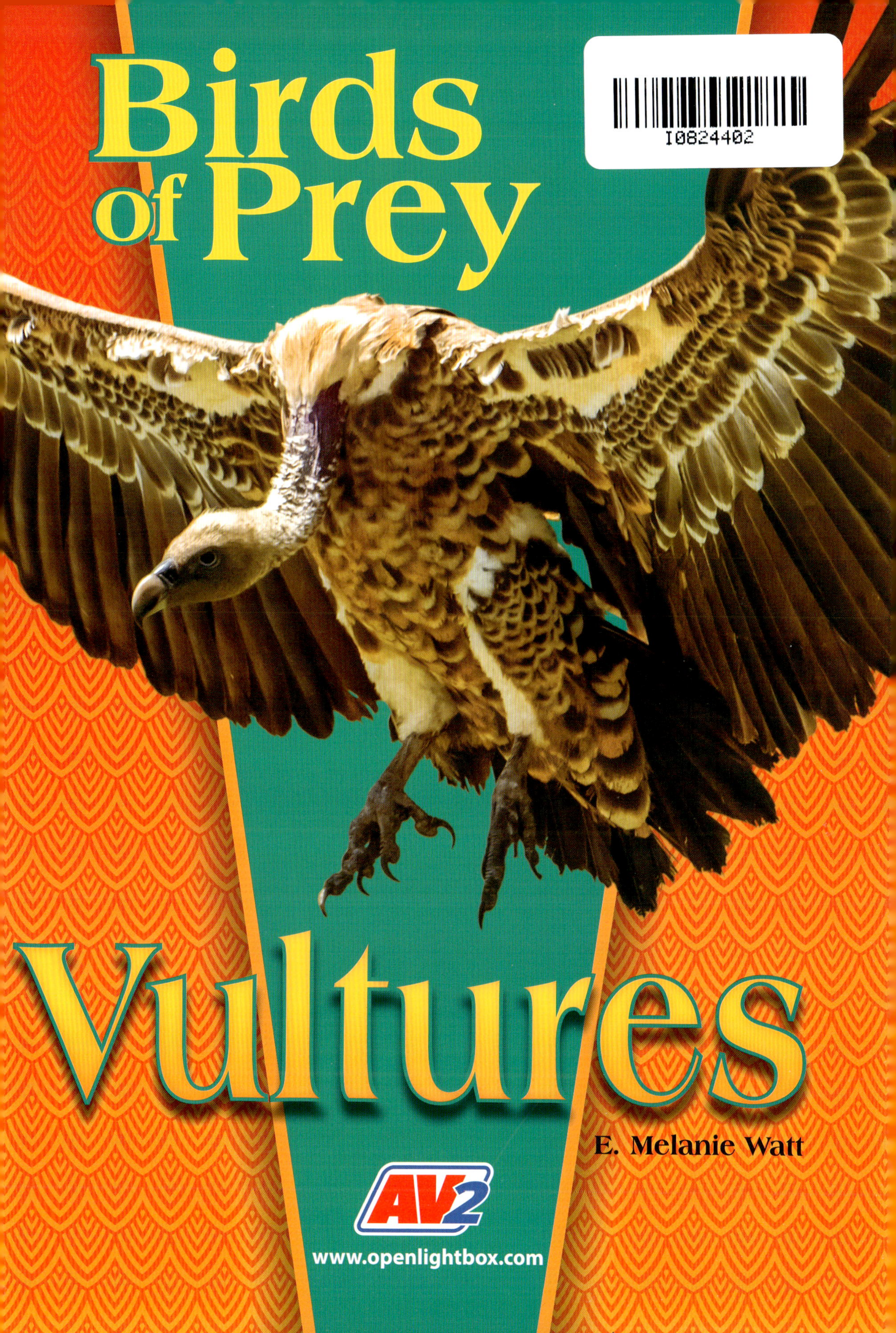

# Birds of Prey

# Vultures

E. Melanie Watt

AV2

www.openlightbox.com

**Step 1**
Go to **www.openlightbox.com**

**Step 2**
Enter this unique code
**FGMJKJCHE**

**Step 3**
Explore your interactive eBook!

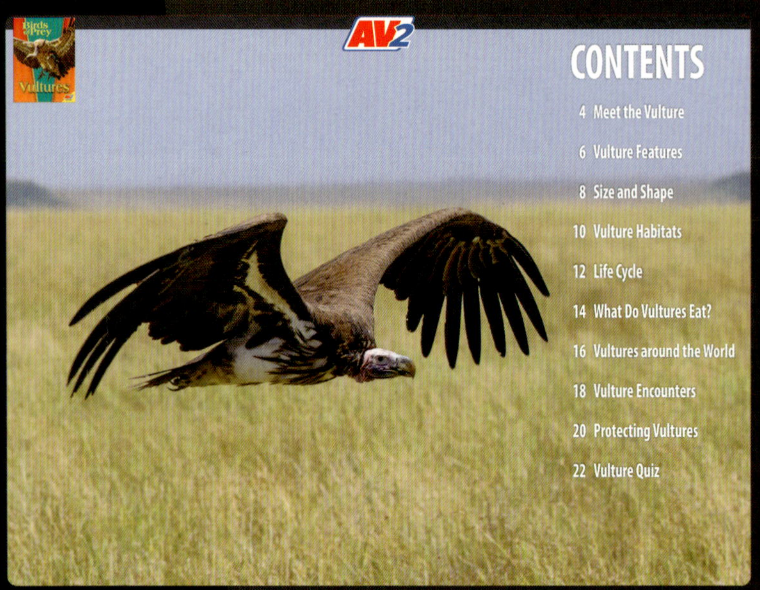


**AV2 is optimized for use on any device**

# Your interactive eBook comes with...

**Contents**
Browse a live contents page to easily navigate through resources

**Audio**
Listen to sections of the book read aloud

**Videos**
Watch informative video clips

**Weblinks**
Gain additional information for research

**Slideshows**
View images and captions

**Try This!**
Complete activities and hands-on experiments

**Key Words**
Study vocabulary, and complete a matching word activity

**Quizzes**
Test your knowledge

**Share**
Share titles within your Learning Management System (LMS) or Library Circulation System

**Citation**
Create bibliographical references following the Chicago Manual of Style

**This title is part of our AV2 digital subscription**

**1-Year K–5 Subscription**
**ISBN** 978-1-7911-3320-7

Access hundreds of AV2 titles with our digital subscription.
Sign up for a FREE trial at **www.openlightbox.com/trial**

## CONTENTS

# Meet the Vulture

Vultures are part of a group of birds known as birds of **prey**, or raptors. This group also includes birds such as eagles and falcons. Vultures are **carnivores**. However, they rarely kill other animals. Instead, they mainly feed on the decaying bodies of dead animals, also known as carrion. Vultures soar through the skies looking for their next meal.

Many vultures have bald or partly-bald heads. Their heavy bodies give them a hunched-over look. Vultures also have hooked beaks and broad wings.

Although many raptors are solitary, vultures are often very social. They fly, feed, and **roost** in groups. For example, Rüppell's griffon vultures **breed** in colonies of up to 1,000 pairs.

# Types of Vultures

Although all vultures **species** share common features, they have a wide range of different shapes, colors, and sizes.

Bearded Vulture

(*Gypaetus barbatus*)

Black Vulture

(*Coragyps atratus*)

California Condor

(*Gymnogyps californianus*)

Egyptian Vulture

(*Neophron percnopterus*)

Hooded Vulture

(*Necrosyrtes monachus*)

King Vulture

(*Sarcoramphus papa*)

Lappet-Faced Vulture

(*Torgos tracheliotos*)

Turkey Vulture

(*Cathartes aura*)

# Vulture Features

Vultures have many **adaptations** that help them find and eat their food. These features include their eyesight and wide **wingspans**.

**HEADS**
The bald or nearly-bald heads of many vultures are thought to help the birds keep clean and control their body temperature.

**BEAK**
Vultures have sharp, hooked beaks. This shape allows them to rip apart meat.

**NOSTRILS**
Some vultures have a very good sense of smell. This helps them to find carrion more easily.

**EYES**
Vultures are able to see carrion, or other vultures circling around carrion, from several miles (kilometers) away.

WINGS
Vultures use their large wings to soar for a long time without needing to spend energy flapping.
Cool Facts
To find food, most vultures in the Americas rely heavily on their vision. Vultures in Europe, Africa, and Asia use both vision and a keen sense of smell to locate carrion.

# Size and Shape

There are 22 species of vultures. They can be split into two groups. The Old World group includes 15 species that live in Africa, Europe, and Asia. The New World group includes 7 species that live in North, Central, and South America. Although they are both called vultures, and are both **scavengers**, the two groups are not closely related.

Old World vultures share several features with eagles and hawks. For instance, they have large, strong, grasping **talons**, and many have feathered heads. Old World vultures can make a number of different sounds, including grunts and squawks.

New World vultures have weak, flat feet that are not suited for grasping. All New World vultures have bald heads. They can only make hissing sounds.

The Andean condor is the heaviest vulture. It can weigh up to 33 pounds (15 kilograms).

# Vulture Wingspans

## Egyptian Vulture
Wingspan
Between 61 and 67 inches (155 and 170 centimeters)

## Turkey Vulture
Wingspan
Between 67 and 72 inches (170 and 183 cm)

## White-Backed Vulture
Wingspan
Between 77 and 89 inches (196 and 226 cm)

## Griffon Vulture
Wingspan
Between 91 and 110 inches (231 and 280 cm)

## Himalayan Griffon Vulture
Wingspan
Between 91 and 118 inches (231 and 300 cm)

## Andean Condor
Wingspan
Up to 130 inches (330 cm)

# Vulture Habitats

Vultures are found on all continents except for Antarctica and Australia. They are adaptable birds. Vultures can survive in many locations, as long as there is carrion to eat. They typically live in **tropical** or subtropical areas.

Vulture **habitats** include grasslands, shrublands, savannas, forests, deserts, wetlands, rocky cliffs, and mountain peaks. Some vultures even live in or around towns and cities. Many species of vulture migrate between habitats. Within these different habitats, vultures need to find food and raise their young.

Lappet-faced vultures are the largest African vultures. They often live in dry areas with few trees where they can use their eyesight to easily spot carrion.

Rüppell's griffon vultures can fly higher than any other bird. One was recorded flying more than 36,000 feet (11,000 meters) above sea level.

## Cool Facts

The name for a group of vultures depends on what the birds are doing. Vultures resting on the ground or in a tree are called a committee. When a group is feeding on carrion, it is called a wake.

# Life Cycle

Many vulture species mate for life. Old World vulture pairs tend to lay their eggs in nests of sticks in trees or on cliffs. They may nest with other vultures in large colonies. New World vulture pairs usually nest on their own. They generally lay their eggs in a hole in a cliff or tree.

## 1 Eggs

The number and size of the eggs a vulture lays depend on its species. Larger vulture species usually lay one egg, while smaller species often lay two. The mated pair work together to look after the eggs.

## 2 Nestlings

Vulture eggs hatch about one to two months after being laid. Newborn vultures, or **nestlings**, are covered in fuzzy feathers called down. Both parents bring their nestlings meat to eat. Nestlings grow quickly. They are ready to **fledge** by the time they are six months old.

## 3 Adults

Depending on the species, vultures can take five to seven years to become adults. Vultures are long-lived birds. Many species can live more than 20 years in nature. In **captivity**, some vultures have lived into their 40s.

# What Do Vultures Eat?

Vultures will sometimes hunt small prey, such as insects, small reptiles, and amphibians. However, they mostly eat dead, rotting animals. Vultures have strong stomach acids that break down this food safely. The acid helps defend the bird from bacteria and viruses. By feeding on carrion, vultures help reduce any diseases it could spread.

Vultures may need to wait weeks between meals. A pouch in a vulture's throat, called a crop, allows the bird to save food for later. A vulture can take large amounts of food from a carcass and store it in its crop.

Different types of vultures can feed on the same meal. When this happens, smaller vultures must wait their turn. They eat what is left behind by the larger birds.

Palm-nut vultures are known for their unusual eating habits. While they will eat some small animals, much of their diet come from the fruit of palm trees.

Bearded vultures mostly eat bones. They swallow small bones whole and drop large bones onto rocks from the air to break them.

# Vultures around the World

Vultures can be found in many different places on Earth. They may eat different types of animals and live in a variety of habitats, but each type of vulture is adapted to survive where it lives.

## CALIFORNIA CONDOR

The California condor is the largest bird in the United States. One of the rarest birds in the world, it was once extinct in the wild. These birds are only found in small areas in California, Utah, Arizona, and the Mexican state of Baja California. Using warm air currents, California condors can soar up to nearly 15,000 feet (4,600 m) with little effort. They may fly 150 miles (240 km) while searching for food.

## TURKEY VULTURE

Turkey vultures are found in South, Central, and North America. Unlike many other New World vultures, they can smell carrion from 8 miles (13 km) away. Turkey vultures were named for their dark feathers and red head. These features make them look like wild turkeys. Their dark feathers take in large amounts of heat. In the morning, turkey vultures will stand with their wings spread to take in heat from the Sun.

## HIMALAYAN GRIFFON VULTURE

Himalayan griffon vultures are found in areas of high land in central Asia, including Kazakhstan, Afghanistan, China, and Mongolia. They eat the carrion of large mammals, including both wildlife and livestock. Due to their huge size, Himalayan griffon vultures scare away many other scavengers when eating. Most other animals will keep away until these birds have eaten their fill.

## EGYPTIAN VULTURE

These small vultures have mostly white feathers, with black on their wings. Their face is bare, with yellow skin. Egyptian vultures are known to use tools. They throw rocks at large eggs, such as ostrich eggs, to break them. Along with carrion and eggs, they eat small animals and waste from larger animals. They are found in many places in Europe, Asia, and Africa. However, their numbers are low. Many people hunt and poison them.

# Vulture Encounters

Although vultures can be very large and have sharp, hooked beaks, they are not often dangerous to humans. However, humans can be very dangerous to them. Some people consider vultures to be pests. This is because vultures can damage buildings. Their waste can also cause health problems.

Vultures may abandon their nests if bothered. In many places, interactions with humans have made certain vulture species **endangered**. In these places, different measures can be taken to prevent vultures from getting close to people. Cleaning up waste, removing dead animals, and using sprinklers or noisemakers are safe ways to keep vultures away.

Many birdwatchers enjoy watching vultures from a distance. People have also set up webcams in vulture nests around the world. This allows people to learn more about these birds without bothering them.

Vultures can help people in many ways. In Lima, the capital city of Peru, black vultures are trained to help people find illegal garbage dumps.

## Cool Facts

A vulture may spit up the food in its stomach to distract an animal that bothers it. This also makes the bird lighter so it can fly away more easily.

# Protecting Vultures

Vulture numbers are dropping for many reasons. These include habitat loss, hunting, and poisoning. Parts of bullets in carcasses left by hunters can make vultures sick. Vultures can also get sick when feeding on dead livestock that have been given medicine. Farmers may also poison pests that are later eaten by vultures.

People protect vultures in many ways. Some governments have passed laws to prevent habitat loss and control the chemicals and poisons people use on livestock and pests. Captive breeding programs, in which vultures are raised in captivity then released into nature as adults, also help increase vulture numbers.

# California Condor Case Study

In the 1980s, only 27 California condors were left in the wild. To help save them, people put all the remaining birds into a captive breeding program. In 1992, the first captive-bred condors were set free. Condors typically lay one egg at a time. However, if the first egg they lay is taken from them, they will lay another. This has allowed scientists to get the birds to lay twice as many eggs. At first, scientists fed the nestlings from the eggs they took using condor-like hand puppets. This made sure the birds would not become used to humans. Today, captive condor pairs help raise the eggs that scientists take. California condors are still critically endangered, but their numbers continue to grow.

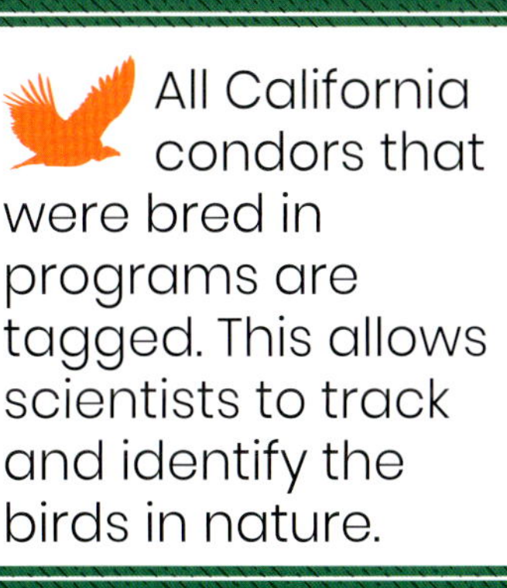

# Vulture Quiz

**1** How high can a California condor soar?

**2** Which species of vulture throws rocks to break open large eggs?

**3** Where do vultures store extra food?

**4** When were the first captive-bred California condors released?

**5** What kind of sounds do New World vultures make?

**6** What do turkey vultures do to warm up in the morning?

**7** How do bald heads help many vultures?

**8** What is a group of vultures called if the birds are resting in a tree?

**Answers:**
**1.** Up to 15,000 feet (4,600 m) **2.** Egyptian vulture **3.** In their crop **4.** 1992
**5.** Hissing sounds **6.** Spread their wings to take in heat from the Sun
**7.** They help keep their heads clean and control their body temperature. **8.** A committee

# Key Words

**adaptations:** changes in living things that help them survive in their environment

**breed:** have young

**captivity:** not living in a natural habitat

**carnivores:** animals that survive by eating meat

**endangered:** in danger of no longer existing anywhere on Earth

**fledge:** become able to fly

**habitats:** places where animals or plants normally live in nature

**nestlings:** birds too young to leave the nest

**prey:** animals that are hunted by other animals for food

**roost:** to rest in a high place

**scavengers:** animals that eat carrion or garbage

**species:** a group of animals with the same characteristics; members of a species can usually only breed with other members of that species

**talons:** sharp claws found on certain birds of prey

**tropical:** a warm area near the equator

**wingspans:** the width of a bird's wings, from tip to tip, when they are spread out

# Index

# Get the best of both worlds.

AV2 bridges the gap between print and digital.

The expandable resources toolbar enables quick access to content including **videos**, **audio**, **activities**, **weblinks**, **slideshows**, **quizzes**, and **key words**.

**Animated videos** make static images come alive.

Resource icons on each page help readers to further **explore key concepts**.

Published by Lightbox Learning Inc.
276 5th Avenue, Suite 704 #917
New York, NY 10001
Website: www.openlightbox.com



Library of Congress Control Number: 2022938862

ISBN 978-1-7911-4715-0 (hardcover)
ISBN 978-1-7911-4716-7 (softcover)
ISBN 978-1-7911-4717-4 (multi-user eBook)

Printed in Guangzhou, China
1 2 3 4 5 6 7 8 9 0 26 25 24 23 22

072022
101121

Project Coordinator: John Willis
Designer: Terry Paulhus

Photo Credits
Every reasonable effort has been made to trace ownership and to obtain permission to reprint copyright material. The publisher would be pleased to have any errors or omissions brought to its attention so that they may be corrected in subsequent printings. The publisher acknowledges Alamy, Minden Pictures, Getty Images, and Shutterstock as its primary image suppliers for this title.